50 Midnight in China Dishes

By: Kelly Johnson

Table of Contents

- Peking Duck
- Xiaolongbao (Soup Dumplings)
- Kung Pao Chicken
- Ma Po Tofu
- Hot Pot with Assorted Meats and Veggies
- Zongzi (Sticky Rice Dumplings)
- Char Siu (BBQ Pork)
- Wontons in Chili Oil
- Scallion Pancakes
- Szechuan Dan Dan Noodles
- Eggplant with Garlic Sauce
- Sweet and Sour Pork
- Cantonese Shrimp with Lobster Sauce
- Lion's Head Meatballs
- Shrimp Toast
- Fried Wontons with Sweet and Sour Sauce
- Beef with Broccoli

- Sautéed Snow Peas with Mushrooms
- Chinese Steamed Buns (Baozi)
- Cantonese Roast Goose
- Fish-Fragrant Pork
- Duck with Orange Sauce
- Chinese-style Braised Pork Belly
- Steamed Fish with Soy and Ginger
- Mongolian Beef
- Dim Sum Platter
- Shandong-Style Chicken
- Stir-Fried Chinese Broccoli (Gai Lan)
- Sichuan Peppercorn Chicken
- Tea-Smoked Duck
- Fried Rice with BBQ Pork
- Lotus Root Stir-Fry
- Sweet Soy Braised Chicken Wings
- Red-braised Pork
- Stir-Fried Clams with Black Bean Sauce
- Chive Dumplings

- Braised Oxtail
- Egg Foo Young
- Chinese Beef Noodle Soup
- Pork and Shrimp Spring Rolls
- Chinese-style Lamb Skewers
- Pineapple Fried Rice
- Stir-Fried Tofu with Shiitake Mushrooms
- Chongqing Hot Chicken
- Spicy Garlic Crab
- Salt and Pepper Squid
- Lo Mein with Vegetables
- Szechuan Shrimp
- Stir-Fried Eggplant with Minced Pork
- Crab Rangoon

Peking Duck

Ingredients:

- 1 whole duck (about 5 lbs)
- 1 tbsp soy sauce
- 1 tbsp hoisin sauce
- 1 tbsp rice vinegar
- 2 tsp sugar
- 1/2 tsp five-spice powder
- 2 tbsp honey
- 2-3 scallions, sliced
- 10-12 Chinese pancakes or steamed buns
- Cucumber, sliced thinly

Instructions:

1. Preheat the oven to 350°F (175°C).
2. Mix soy sauce, hoisin sauce, rice vinegar, sugar, and five-spice powder to create the marinade.
3. Rub the duck with the marinade, making sure to coat it evenly. Let marinate in the refrigerator for at least 2 hours or overnight.
4. Roast the duck for about 1.5 hours, basting with honey every 30 minutes, until the skin is crispy and golden.
5. Let the duck rest for 10 minutes before carving.

6. Serve with Chinese pancakes, sliced scallions, cucumber, and hoisin sauce.

Xiaolongbao (Soup Dumplings)

Ingredients:

- 2 cups all-purpose flour
- 3/4 cup warm water
- 1/2 lb ground pork
- 1/4 cup gelatin, dissolved in 1/2 cup warm water
- 2 tbsp soy sauce
- 1 tbsp rice wine
- 1 tbsp ginger, minced
- 1 tsp sesame oil
- Salt to taste

Instructions:

1. Make the dough by mixing flour and warm water. Knead until smooth and let rest for 30 minutes.
2. Combine ground pork, gelatin mixture, soy sauce, rice wine, ginger, sesame oil, and salt to create the filling.
3. Roll the dough into small balls and flatten into circles. Place a spoonful of filling in the center, then pleat the edges and seal the dumpling.
4. Steam the dumplings in a bamboo steamer for about 8-10 minutes.
5. Serve immediately, dipping in soy sauce or vinegar.

Kung Pao Chicken

Ingredients:

- 1 lb chicken breast, diced
- 1/4 cup roasted peanuts
- 2 tbsp soy sauce
- 1 tbsp rice vinegar
- 1 tbsp hoisin sauce
- 1 tbsp sugar
- 1 tbsp sesame oil
- 2-3 dried red chilies
- 3-4 cloves garlic, minced
- 1 tbsp ginger, minced
- 1/2 bell pepper, diced
- 1/2 onion, diced
- 2 tbsp green onions, sliced

Instructions:

1. In a bowl, mix soy sauce, rice vinegar, hoisin sauce, sugar, and sesame oil to create the sauce.
2. Heat a pan or wok and sauté the dried chilies, garlic, and ginger until fragrant.
3. Add chicken and cook until browned and cooked through.

4. Add the bell pepper, onion, and sauce mixture. Stir-fry for 3-4 minutes.

5. Toss in peanuts and green onions, then serve hot with steamed rice.

Ma Po Tofu

Ingredients:

- 1 block firm tofu, cut into cubes
- 1/2 lb ground pork
- 2 tbsp soy sauce
- 1 tbsp fermented black beans, chopped
- 1 tbsp Sichuan peppercorns, ground
- 2 tbsp chili paste
- 1 tbsp rice wine
- 1 tsp sugar
- 2-3 green onions, chopped
- 1 tbsp cornstarch mixed with 2 tbsp water
- 1 tbsp sesame oil

Instructions:

1. Heat sesame oil in a pan and sauté ground pork until browned.
2. Add fermented black beans, Sichuan peppercorns, chili paste, and rice wine. Stir to combine.
3. Add tofu cubes and cook for 5-6 minutes, adding soy sauce and sugar.
4. Stir in the cornstarch mixture to thicken the sauce. Cook for another 2-3 minutes.
5. Garnish with chopped green onions and serve with steamed rice.

Hot Pot with Assorted Meats and Veggies

Ingredients:

- 4 cups chicken or beef broth
- 2 tbsp soy sauce
- 1 tbsp rice vinegar
- 1 tbsp sesame oil
- 1 tbsp chili paste (optional)
- 1/2 lb thinly sliced beef, pork, and lamb
- Assorted vegetables (mushrooms, bok choy, napa cabbage, spinach)
- Tofu cubes
- Noodles (optional)

Instructions:

1. In a large pot, combine chicken broth, soy sauce, rice vinegar, sesame oil, and chili paste. Bring to a simmer.
2. Add sliced meats and vegetables to the pot, cooking for 2-3 minutes until tender.
3. Optionally, add tofu and noodles. Let cook for another 5 minutes.
4. Serve the hot pot with dipping sauces on the side.

Zongzi (Sticky Rice Dumplings)

Ingredients:

- 2 cups glutinous rice, soaked for 4 hours
- 10-12 bamboo leaves, soaked and softened
- 1/2 lb pork belly, cut into cubes
- 1/4 cup dried shrimp, soaked
- 1/4 cup shiitake mushrooms, soaked and sliced
- 2 tbsp soy sauce
- 1 tbsp five-spice powder
- 1 tbsp oyster sauce
- Salt and pepper to taste

Instructions:

1. Mix pork, dried shrimp, mushrooms, soy sauce, five-spice powder, oyster sauce, salt, and pepper in a bowl.
2. Place a soaked bamboo leaf on a flat surface. Add a spoonful of soaked rice, followed by the filling, and top with another spoonful of rice.
3. Fold the leaves into a pyramid shape and tie with string.
4. Steam the zongzi for 2–3 hours, checking the water level periodically.
5. Serve warm.

Char Siu (BBQ Pork)

Ingredients:

- 1 lb pork shoulder or pork belly
- 2 tbsp hoisin sauce
- 2 tbsp soy sauce
- 2 tbsp sugar
- 1 tbsp rice wine
- 1 tbsp honey
- 1/2 tsp five-spice powder
- 1/4 tsp red food coloring (optional)

Instructions:

1. Mix hoisin sauce, soy sauce, sugar, rice wine, honey, five-spice powder, and food coloring in a bowl.
2. Marinate the pork in the sauce for at least 2 hours or overnight.
3. Preheat the oven to 375°F (190°C). Place the pork on a rack in a roasting pan.
4. Roast the pork for 45-50 minutes, basting every 15 minutes with the marinade.
5. Slice and serve with rice or in bao buns.

Wontons in Chili Oil

Ingredients:

- 20 wonton wrappers
- 1/2 lb ground pork
- 1 tbsp soy sauce
- 1 tbsp ginger, minced
- 1 tsp sesame oil
- 2 tbsp chili oil
- 1 tbsp soy sauce
- 2 garlic cloves, minced
- 1 tbsp sugar
- 1/4 tsp Sichuan peppercorns, ground

Instructions:

1. Mix ground pork, soy sauce, ginger, and sesame oil. Place a small spoonful in each wonton wrapper and fold into triangles.
2. Boil the wontons for about 5 minutes until they float.
3. In a pan, heat chili oil, soy sauce, garlic, sugar, and Sichuan peppercorns. Stir well.
4. Pour the chili oil sauce over the cooked wontons and serve.

Scallion Pancakes

Ingredients:

- 2 cups all-purpose flour
- 1/2 cup boiling water
- 1/4 cup sesame oil
- 4 scallions, chopped
- Salt to taste

Instructions:

1. Mix flour and boiling water until a dough forms. Knead until smooth and let rest for 30 minutes.
2. Roll the dough into a thin circle and brush with sesame oil. Sprinkle with scallions and salt.
3. Roll the dough up like a log, then coil it into a ball. Flatten the ball into a pancake.
4. Fry the pancake in a hot pan with oil for 2–3 minutes per side until golden brown and crispy.
5. Slice and serve.

Szechuan Dan Dan Noodles

Ingredients:

- 4 oz noodles (Chinese egg noodles)
- 1/2 lb ground pork
- 2 tbsp soy sauce
- 1 tbsp sesame paste or peanut butter
- 1 tbsp chili oil
- 1 tbsp rice vinegar
- 1 tbsp sugar
- 1/2 tsp Sichuan peppercorns, ground
- 2-3 green onions, chopped

Instructions:

1. Cook noodles according to package instructions and set aside.
2. In a pan, sauté ground pork until browned. Add soy sauce, sesame paste, chili oil, rice vinegar, and sugar. Stir to combine.
3. Toss the cooked noodles with the sauce mixture.
4. Garnish with ground Sichuan peppercorns and chopped green onions before serving.

Eggplant with Garlic Sauce

Ingredients:

- 2 medium eggplants, cut into bite-sized pieces
- 3 tbsp soy sauce
- 2 tbsp rice vinegar
- 1 tbsp hoisin sauce
- 1 tbsp sugar
- 2 tbsp vegetable oil
- 3 garlic cloves, minced
- 1 tbsp ginger, minced
- 2 green onions, chopped
- 1 tsp chili paste or sauce (optional)

Instructions:

1. Heat vegetable oil in a pan and fry the eggplant pieces until golden and tender. Set aside.
2. In the same pan, sauté garlic and ginger until fragrant, about 1-2 minutes.
3. Add soy sauce, rice vinegar, hoisin sauce, sugar, and chili paste. Stir to combine and cook for another 2-3 minutes.
4. Return the fried eggplant to the pan and toss to coat evenly with the sauce.
5. Garnish with chopped green onions and serve hot.

Sweet and Sour Pork

Ingredients:

- 1 lb pork tenderloin, cut into bite-sized pieces
- 1/4 cup cornstarch
- 1/2 cup flour
- 1 egg, beaten
- 1 cup vegetable oil (for frying)
- 1/2 cup pineapple chunks
- 1/2 onion, diced
- 1/2 bell pepper, diced
- 1/2 cup vinegar
- 1/2 cup sugar
- 1/4 cup ketchup
- 1 tbsp soy sauce

Instructions:

1. Mix cornstarch and flour in a bowl. Dip the pork pieces into the beaten egg, then coat in the flour mixture.

2. Heat vegetable oil in a pan and fry the pork pieces until golden and crispy. Remove and drain excess oil on paper towels.

3. In a separate pan, combine vinegar, sugar, ketchup, soy sauce, and a little water. Bring to a boil, stirring to dissolve the sugar.

4. Add onion, bell pepper, and pineapple chunks to the sauce. Simmer for 3-4 minutes.

5. Toss the fried pork into the sauce and stir to coat.

6. Serve hot with steamed rice.

Cantonese Shrimp with Lobster Sauce

Ingredients:

- 1 lb shrimp, peeled and deveined
- 2 tbsp vegetable oil
- 2 garlic cloves, minced
- 1/4 cup fermented black beans, rinsed and chopped
- 1/4 cup chicken broth
- 1 tbsp soy sauce
- 1 tbsp rice wine
- 1/2 tsp sugar
- 1 tbsp cornstarch mixed with 2 tbsp water
- 2 green onions, chopped
- 1/4 cup lobster stock or clam juice (optional)

Instructions:

1. Heat vegetable oil in a pan and sauté garlic and fermented black beans until fragrant.
2. Add the shrimp and cook until they turn pink, about 2-3 minutes.
3. Stir in the chicken broth, soy sauce, rice wine, sugar, and lobster stock (if using).
4. Add the cornstarch mixture and stir until the sauce thickens.
5. Garnish with chopped green onions and serve with rice.

Lion's Head Meatballs

Ingredients:

- 1 lb ground pork
- 1/4 cup water chestnuts, chopped
- 1 egg
- 1/4 cup ginger, minced
- 2 tbsp soy sauce
- 2 tbsp rice wine
- 1/4 tsp sesame oil
- 1 tbsp cornstarch
- 1 tbsp sugar
- 4 cups chicken broth
- 2 bok choy, chopped

Instructions:

1. Mix ground pork, water chestnuts, egg, ginger, soy sauce, rice wine, sesame oil, cornstarch, and sugar in a bowl. Form the mixture into large meatballs.

2. Heat a pot of chicken broth to a simmer. Gently drop the meatballs into the broth and cook for 15-20 minutes until cooked through.

3. Add bok choy and cook for an additional 5 minutes.

4. Serve the meatballs in the broth with some of the bok choy.

Shrimp Toast

Ingredients:

- 1/2 lb shrimp, peeled and deveined
- 2 tbsp soy sauce
- 1 egg white
- 2 tbsp cornstarch
- 4 slices white bread, crusts removed
- 1/4 cup sesame oil
- 2 tbsp chopped green onions

Instructions:

1. Blend the shrimp, soy sauce, egg white, and cornstarch in a food processor until smooth.
2. Spread the shrimp mixture on the bread slices.
3. Heat sesame oil in a pan over medium heat and fry the bread slices, shrimp side down, until golden brown and crispy.
4. Garnish with chopped green onions and serve immediately.

Fried Wontons with Sweet and Sour Sauce

Ingredients:

- 1 package wonton wrappers
- 1/2 lb ground pork
- 2 tbsp soy sauce
- 1 tbsp sesame oil
- 1/4 cup chopped green onions
- 1/4 tsp ground ginger
- 1 egg, beaten
- Vegetable oil for frying
- For the sauce: 1/4 cup ketchup, 2 tbsp vinegar, 1/4 cup sugar, 1 tbsp soy sauce

Instructions:

1. Combine ground pork, soy sauce, sesame oil, green onions, and ginger in a bowl. Place a teaspoon of filling in each wonton wrapper, fold, and seal with egg wash.

2. Heat vegetable oil in a pan and fry the wontons until golden and crispy, about 2-3 minutes per side.

3. For the sauce: Combine ketchup, vinegar, sugar, and soy sauce in a small saucepan. Bring to a boil and simmer for 2-3 minutes.

4. Serve the wontons with the sweet and sour dipping sauce.

Beef with Broccoli

Ingredients:

- 1 lb flank steak, thinly sliced
- 2 cups broccoli florets
- 2 tbsp soy sauce
- 1 tbsp oyster sauce
- 1 tbsp sesame oil
- 1 tbsp cornstarch
- 2 tbsp vegetable oil
- 2 garlic cloves, minced
- 1/2 cup beef broth

Instructions:

1. In a bowl, mix soy sauce, oyster sauce, sesame oil, and cornstarch. Add the sliced beef and marinate for 15-20 minutes.
2. Heat vegetable oil in a pan and sauté garlic until fragrant.
3. Add the beef and cook for 2-3 minutes, then add the broccoli and beef broth.
4. Stir-fry until the broccoli is tender and the beef is cooked through, about 5-7 minutes.
5. Serve hot with steamed rice.

Sautéed Snow Peas with Mushrooms

Ingredients:

- 2 cups snow peas, trimmed
- 1 cup mushrooms, sliced
- 1 tbsp soy sauce
- 1 tbsp sesame oil
- 1 garlic clove, minced
- 1 tbsp rice vinegar

Instructions:

1. Heat sesame oil in a pan and sauté garlic until fragrant.
2. Add mushrooms and cook for 3-4 minutes until tender.
3. Stir in snow peas and soy sauce, then cook for another 3-4 minutes.
4. Add rice vinegar and toss to coat. Serve hot.

Chinese Steamed Buns (Baozi)

Ingredients:

- For the dough:
    - 2 cups all-purpose flour
    - 1/4 cup sugar
    - 2 tsp baking powder
    - 1/2 cup warm water
    - 1 tbsp active dry yeast
- For the filling:
    - 1/2 lb ground pork
    - 2 tbsp soy sauce
    - 1 tbsp hoisin sauce
    - 1/4 tsp five-spice powder
    - 2 green onions, chopped

Instructions:

1. Mix flour, sugar, baking powder, and yeast in a bowl. Add warm water and knead into a smooth dough. Let it rise for 1-2 hours.
2. For the filling, combine ground pork, soy sauce, hoisin sauce, five-spice powder, and green onions.
3. Roll dough into small balls, flatten, and place a spoonful of filling in the center. Pinch the dough to seal.

4. Steam the buns in a bamboo steamer for about 10-15 minutes.

5. Serve hot.

Cantonese Roast Goose

Ingredients:

- 1 whole goose (about 5-6 lbs)
- 2 tbsp soy sauce
- 2 tbsp hoisin sauce
- 1 tbsp rice wine
- 1 tbsp sugar
- 1/4 tsp five-spice powder
- 1/4 tsp Chinese five-spice powder
- 1/2 cup water

Instructions:

1. Preheat the oven to 375°F (190°C).
2. Rub the goose with soy sauce, hoisin sauce, rice wine, sugar, and five-spice powder. Let it marinate for at least 2 hours.
3. Roast the goose for 2–2.5 hours, basting every 30 minutes.
4. Let the goose rest for 15 minutes before carving and serving.

Fish-Fragrant Pork

Ingredients:

- 1 lb ground pork
- 2 tbsp soy sauce
- 2 tbsp rice vinegar
- 1 tbsp sugar
- 1 tbsp fermented chili bean paste (doubanjiang)
- 2 tbsp vegetable oil
- 3 garlic cloves, minced
- 1-inch piece ginger, minced
- 2-3 dried red chilies
- 1/2 cup chicken broth
- 2 green onions, chopped
- 1 tbsp cornstarch mixed with 2 tbsp water (optional, for thickening)

Instructions:

1. Heat oil in a wok and stir-fry the garlic, ginger, and dried chilies until fragrant, about 1 minute.
2. Add the ground pork and cook until browned.
3. Stir in soy sauce, rice vinegar, sugar, and chili bean paste. Cook for another 2 minutes.

4. Add chicken broth and bring to a simmer. If you prefer a thicker sauce, stir in the cornstarch slurry and cook for another minute.

5. Garnish with green onions and serve with steamed rice.

Duck with Orange Sauce

Ingredients:

- 2 duck breasts
- Salt and pepper to taste
- 1/4 cup orange juice
- 1/4 cup soy sauce
- 2 tbsp honey
- 2 tbsp rice vinegar
- 1 tbsp cornstarch (optional, for thickening)
- Zest of 1 orange
- 1-inch piece of ginger, minced
- 2 garlic cloves, minced
- 1 tbsp sesame oil

Instructions:

1. Score the skin of the duck breasts and season with salt and pepper.
2. Heat a skillet over medium-high heat. Cook the duck breasts, skin-side down, for about 5-7 minutes until the skin is crispy. Flip and cook for another 5 minutes for medium rare, or longer for desired doneness.
3. Remove the duck from the pan and let it rest.
4. In the same skillet, sauté garlic, ginger, and orange zest in sesame oil until fragrant.

5. Add orange juice, soy sauce, honey, and rice vinegar. Simmer for 5 minutes, reducing the sauce slightly.

6. If a thicker sauce is desired, mix cornstarch with a little water and stir it into the sauce. Simmer for another 2-3 minutes.

7. Slice the duck breasts and drizzle with the orange sauce before serving.

Chinese-style Braised Pork Belly

Ingredients:

- 2 lb pork belly, cut into 2-inch cubes
- 2 tbsp soy sauce
- 2 tbsp dark soy sauce
- 2 tbsp rice wine
- 1 tbsp sugar
- 1 cinnamon stick
- 3-4 star anise
- 1-inch piece ginger, sliced
- 3-4 cloves garlic, smashed
- 1/2 cup chicken broth
- 1 tbsp sesame oil

Instructions:

1. Blanch the pork belly cubes in boiling water for 5 minutes to remove impurities. Drain and set aside.
2. Heat sesame oil in a pot over medium heat. Add the pork belly and cook until browned on all sides.
3. Add soy sauce, dark soy sauce, rice wine, sugar, ginger, garlic, cinnamon stick, and star anise. Stir to combine.

4. Add chicken broth and bring to a simmer. Cover and braise for 1.5-2 hours, until the pork is tender and the sauce has thickened.

5. Serve hot with steamed rice.

Steamed Fish with Soy and Ginger

Ingredients:

- 1 whole fish (such as tilapia, sea bass, or snapper), cleaned and scaled
- 2 tbsp soy sauce
- 1 tbsp rice wine
- 1 tbsp sesame oil
- 3-4 slices of ginger
- 2-3 green onions, sliced
- 1 tbsp cilantro, chopped (optional)

Instructions:

1. Place the fish on a heatproof plate. Scatter ginger slices inside the fish cavity and top with some green onions.
2. In a small bowl, mix soy sauce, rice wine, and sesame oil. Pour over the fish.
3. Set the plate in a steamer and steam the fish for 12-15 minutes, or until the fish is fully cooked and flakes easily.
4. Garnish with remaining green onions and cilantro before serving.

Mongolian Beef

Ingredients:

- 1 lb flank steak, thinly sliced against the grain
- 2 tbsp soy sauce
- 2 tbsp hoisin sauce
- 2 tbsp oyster sauce
- 1 tbsp sugar
- 1 tbsp cornstarch
- 2 tbsp vegetable oil
- 2 garlic cloves, minced
- 1-inch piece ginger, minced
- 2-3 dried red chilies
- 2 green onions, chopped

Instructions:

1. In a bowl, mix soy sauce, hoisin sauce, oyster sauce, sugar, and cornstarch. Toss the sliced beef in the sauce and let it marinate for 20 minutes.
2. Heat vegetable oil in a wok or pan over high heat. Stir-fry the garlic, ginger, and dried chilies for 1 minute.
3. Add the marinated beef and cook until browned, about 2-3 minutes.
4. Add green onions and cook for another minute.

5. Serve hot with steamed rice.

Dim Sum Platter

Ingredients (for various dim sum items):

- Dumplings (pork, shrimp, or vegetarian)
- Steamed buns (char siu bao)
- Spring rolls (fried)
- Siu mai (pork and shrimp dumplings)
- Chashu pork buns
- For dipping sauce: soy sauce, rice vinegar, chili oil

Instructions:

1. Prepare each dim sum item according to the specific recipe (e.g., steam dumplings, fry spring rolls, steam buns).
2. Arrange the dim sum items on a large platter.
3. Serve with soy sauce, rice vinegar, and chili oil on the side for dipping.

Shandong-Style Chicken

Ingredients:

- 1 whole chicken, cut into pieces
- 2 tbsp soy sauce
- 1 tbsp rice vinegar
- 1 tbsp sesame oil
- 2 tbsp chili oil
- 2 tbsp sugar
- 1-inch piece ginger, minced
- 3-4 garlic cloves, minced
- 2 tbsp soy bean paste (or miso paste)
- 1/4 cup chicken broth
- 2-3 green onions, chopped

Instructions:

1. Boil the chicken pieces in water for 30-40 minutes, or until cooked through and tender.
2. In a separate pan, heat sesame oil and sauté ginger, garlic, and chili oil for 2 minutes.
3. Add soy sauce, rice vinegar, soy bean paste, sugar, and chicken broth. Stir to combine and cook for 5-7 minutes.
4. Toss the boiled chicken in the sauce and simmer for another 10 minutes.

5. Garnish with green onions and serve with steamed rice.

Stir-Fried Chinese Broccoli (Gai Lan)

Ingredients:

- 1 lb Chinese broccoli (gai lan), trimmed
- 2 tbsp vegetable oil
- 2 garlic cloves, minced
- 1 tbsp oyster sauce
- 1 tbsp soy sauce
- 1/2 cup chicken broth

Instructions:

1. Blanch the gai lan in boiling water for 1-2 minutes, then drain.
2. Heat vegetable oil in a pan and sauté garlic until fragrant.
3. Add the blanched gai lan to the pan and stir-fry for 2 minutes.
4. Stir in oyster sauce, soy sauce, and chicken broth. Cook for another 2-3 minutes until the sauce reduces slightly.
5. Serve hot.

Sichuan Peppercorn Chicken

Ingredients:

- 1 lb boneless chicken thighs, cut into bite-sized pieces
- 2 tbsp soy sauce
- 1 tbsp rice vinegar
- 1 tbsp sugar
- 1 tbsp cornstarch
- 1 tbsp vegetable oil
- 2 tbsp Sichuan peppercorns
- 3-4 dried red chilies
- 2 garlic cloves, minced
- 1-inch piece ginger, minced
- 1 tbsp soy bean paste

Instructions:

1. Marinate the chicken with soy sauce, rice vinegar, sugar, and cornstarch for 20 minutes.
2. Heat vegetable oil in a pan and stir-fry Sichuan peppercorns and dried chilies until fragrant.
3. Add garlic, ginger, and soy bean paste, and cook for 1 minute.
4. Add the marinated chicken and stir-fry until cooked through, about 5-7 minutes.

5. Serve hot with steamed rice.

Tea-Smoked Duck

Ingredients:

- 1 whole duck, cleaned and patted dry
- 2 tbsp soy sauce
- 1 tbsp honey
- 1 tbsp rice wine
- 1 tbsp five-spice powder
- 1 tbsp sugar
- 1/2 cup tea leaves (black tea or green tea)
- 1/4 cup uncooked rice
- 1/4 cup brown sugar
- 2 tbsp sesame oil

Instructions:

1. Rub the duck with soy sauce, honey, rice wine, five-spice powder, and sugar. Marinate for 2 hours.
2. Prepare the smoking mixture: combine tea leaves, rice, and brown sugar in a wok or large pan. Heat over low heat until the mixture begins to smoke.
3. Place the duck on a rack above the smoking mixture and cover with a lid. Smoke for 30-40 minutes.
4. Once smoked, heat sesame oil in a pan and sear the duck on all sides until crispy.
5. Serve hot with steamed rice and vegetables.

Fried Rice with BBQ Pork

Ingredients:

- 2 cups cooked jasmine rice (preferably day-old)
- 1 cup BBQ pork, thinly sliced
- 2 eggs, beaten
- 1/2 cup peas and carrots
- 1/2 onion, chopped
- 2-3 garlic cloves, minced
- 2-3 green onions, chopped
- 2 tbsp soy sauce
- 1 tbsp oyster sauce
- 1 tbsp sesame oil
- 1 tbsp vegetable oil

Instructions:

1. Heat vegetable oil in a wok over medium-high heat. Add onions and garlic, cooking until fragrant.
2. Add the BBQ pork and cook for 2 minutes until warmed through.
3. Push the pork mixture to the side of the wok and pour in the beaten eggs. Scramble them until fully cooked.
4. Add the peas and carrots, followed by the day-old rice. Stir to combine.

5. Stir in soy sauce, oyster sauce, and sesame oil, mixing everything thoroughly.

6. Garnish with chopped green onions and serve hot.

Lotus Root Stir-Fry

Ingredients:

- 1 lotus root, peeled and thinly sliced
- 1 red bell pepper, sliced
- 1 green bell pepper, sliced
- 2-3 garlic cloves, minced
- 2 tbsp soy sauce
- 1 tbsp rice vinegar
- 1 tbsp sugar
- 1 tbsp sesame oil
- 1 tbsp vegetable oil
- 1 tbsp chili paste (optional, for heat)
- 1 tbsp sesame seeds (optional)

Instructions:

1. Heat vegetable oil in a wok over medium-high heat. Add garlic and stir-fry until fragrant.
2. Add the lotus root and stir-fry for about 3-5 minutes until tender but still slightly crisp.
3. Add the bell peppers and cook for another 2 minutes.
4. Stir in soy sauce, rice vinegar, sugar, and chili paste (if using). Stir to combine and cook for another 2-3 minutes.

5. Drizzle with sesame oil, toss to coat, and garnish with sesame seeds if desired. Serve hot.

Sweet Soy Braised Chicken Wings

Ingredients:

- 10 chicken wings
- 2 tbsp soy sauce
- 2 tbsp dark soy sauce
- 2 tbsp sugar
- 2 tbsp rice vinegar
- 1-inch piece ginger, sliced
- 2 garlic cloves, smashed
- 1/2 cup water
- 1 tbsp sesame oil
- 1 tbsp chopped green onions (for garnish)

Instructions:

1. Heat sesame oil in a pan over medium heat. Add garlic and ginger, cooking until fragrant.
2. Add chicken wings and cook until browned on both sides.
3. Stir in soy sauce, dark soy sauce, sugar, rice vinegar, and water. Bring to a simmer.
4. Cover and braise the wings for 25-30 minutes, occasionally flipping them, until they are tender and the sauce thickens.
5. Garnish with chopped green onions and serve with rice.

Red-braised Pork

Ingredients:

- 1 lb pork belly, cut into chunks
- 2 tbsp soy sauce
- 2 tbsp dark soy sauce
- 2 tbsp sugar
- 1 tbsp rice wine
- 2 star anise
- 1 cinnamon stick
- 2-3 cloves garlic, smashed
- 1-inch piece ginger, sliced
- 1/2 cup water

Instructions:

1. Heat oil in a pot over medium-high heat. Add pork belly and cook until browned on all sides.
2. Add soy sauce, dark soy sauce, sugar, rice wine, garlic, ginger, star anise, and cinnamon stick. Stir to combine.
3. Pour in water and bring to a boil. Reduce heat to low, cover, and simmer for 1.5 to 2 hours until the pork is tender and the sauce thickens.
4. Serve with steamed rice.

Stir-Fried Clams with Black Bean Sauce

Ingredients:

- 1 lb fresh clams, scrubbed clean
- 2 tbsp fermented black beans, rinsed and chopped
- 2 tbsp soy sauce
- 1 tbsp rice wine
- 2-3 garlic cloves, minced
- 1-inch piece ginger, minced
- 1/2 onion, chopped
- 2 green onions, chopped
- 1 tbsp vegetable oil

Instructions:

1. Heat vegetable oil in a wok over medium-high heat. Add garlic, ginger, and onion, cooking until fragrant.
2. Stir in fermented black beans and cook for another 1-2 minutes.
3. Add the clams and soy sauce, stirring to coat. Cover and cook for 5-7 minutes until the clams open.
4. Stir in rice wine and cook for an additional 2 minutes.
5. Garnish with green onions and serve immediately.

Chive Dumplings

Ingredients (for dough):

- 2 cups all-purpose flour
- 1/2 cup warm water
- Pinch of salt

Ingredients (for filling):

- 1 bunch chives, finely chopped
- 1/2 lb ground pork
- 2 tbsp soy sauce
- 1 tbsp sesame oil
- 1 tbsp ginger, minced
- 1 garlic clove, minced
- 1 tbsp rice vinegar

Instructions:

1. Mix flour and salt in a bowl, slowly adding warm water to form a dough. Knead until smooth. Let it rest for 30 minutes.

2. For the filling, combine chives, ground pork, soy sauce, sesame oil, ginger, garlic, and rice vinegar in a bowl.

3. Roll out the dough and cut into small circles. Place a spoonful of filling in the center of each circle.

4. Fold the dough over the filling and pinch the edges to seal. Steam the dumplings for 10-12 minutes.

5. Serve with soy sauce for dipping.

Braised Oxtail

Ingredients:

- 2 lbs oxtail, cut into sections
- 2 tbsp soy sauce
- 1 tbsp dark soy sauce
- 1 tbsp sugar
- 1 tbsp rice wine
- 1-inch piece ginger, sliced
- 2 garlic cloves, smashed
- 2 star anise
- 2 cups beef broth
- 2 tbsp vegetable oil

Instructions:

1. Heat vegetable oil in a pot and brown the oxtail sections on all sides.
2. Add soy sauce, dark soy sauce, sugar, rice wine, garlic, ginger, and star anise.
3. Pour in beef broth and bring to a boil. Reduce heat to low, cover, and braise for 2-3 hours until the oxtail is tender.
4. Serve hot with steamed rice.

Egg Foo Young

Ingredients:

- 4 eggs, beaten
- 1/2 cup cooked shrimp, chopped
- 1/2 cup cooked chicken, chopped
- 1/2 cup bean sprouts
- 2-3 green onions, chopped
- 1 tbsp soy sauce
- 1 tbsp cornstarch (optional)
- 1/2 cup vegetable oil
- 1/2 cup chicken broth
- 1 tbsp soy sauce
- 1 tsp sugar
- 1 tsp cornstarch

Instructions:

1. Mix the beaten eggs with shrimp, chicken, bean sprouts, green onions, soy sauce, and cornstarch (if using).
2. Heat vegetable oil in a frying pan over medium heat. Pour in the egg mixture to form a pancake.
3. Cook until golden brown on both sides, about 2-3 minutes per side.

4. For the gravy, combine chicken broth, soy sauce, sugar, and cornstarch in a pan and cook until thickened.

5. Pour the gravy over the egg foo young and serve.

Chinese Beef Noodle Soup

Ingredients:

- 1 lb beef brisket, cut into chunks
- 1 tbsp soy sauce
- 1 tbsp dark soy sauce
- 1 tbsp rice wine
- 2-3 garlic cloves, minced
- 1-inch piece ginger, minced
- 1 tbsp five-spice powder
- 2-3 star anise
- 4 cups beef broth
- 4 oz Chinese wheat noodles
- 2-3 green onions, chopped

Instructions:

1. Brown beef brisket in a pot over medium heat.
2. Add soy sauce, dark soy sauce, rice wine, garlic, ginger, five-spice powder, and star anise. Stir to combine.
3. Add beef broth and bring to a boil. Reduce heat and simmer for 2-3 hours until the beef is tender.
4. Cook the noodles according to package instructions.

5. Serve the beef and broth over the noodles, garnished with green onions.

Pork and Shrimp Spring Rolls

Ingredients:

- 1/2 lb ground pork
- 1/2 lb shrimp, peeled and chopped
- 1 cup shredded cabbage
- 1/2 cup carrots, shredded
- 2-3 garlic cloves, minced
- 1 tbsp soy sauce
- 1 tsp sesame oil
- 1 tsp cornstarch
- 10 spring roll wrappers
- Vegetable oil for frying

Instructions:

1. Heat vegetable oil in a pan and cook the ground pork until browned.
2. Add shrimp, garlic, soy sauce, sesame oil, and cornstarch. Cook until the shrimp turns pink.
3. Stir in shredded cabbage and carrots and cook until tender.
4. Place a spoonful of filling in each spring roll wrapper and roll tightly, sealing the edges.
5. Heat oil in a pan and fry the spring rolls until golden and crispy. Serve with dipping sauce.

Chinese-style Lamb Skewers

Ingredients:

- 1 lb lamb, cut into small cubes
- 1 tbsp soy sauce
- 1 tbsp rice wine
- 1 tsp ground cumin
- 1 tsp ground coriander
- 1 tbsp chili powder
- 2 tbsp vegetable oil
- Skewers (wooden or metal)

Instructions:

1. In a bowl, combine soy sauce, rice wine, cumin, coriander, chili powder, and vegetable oil. Marinate the lamb cubes for at least 30 minutes.
2. Thread the lamb onto skewers.
3. Grill or cook the skewers over medium-high heat for 5-7 minutes, turning occasionally, until the lamb is browned and cooked through.
4. Serve with flatbread or steamed rice.

Pineapple Fried Rice

Ingredients:

- 2 cups cooked jasmine rice (preferably day-old)
- 1/2 cup cooked chicken, diced
- 1/2 cup shrimp, peeled and deveined
- 1/2 cup pineapple chunks (fresh or canned)
- 1/2 cup peas and carrots
- 1/4 cup cashews or peanuts
- 2 eggs, lightly beaten
- 2-3 garlic cloves, minced
- 2 green onions, chopped
- 2 tbsp soy sauce
- 1 tbsp fish sauce
- 1 tbsp oyster sauce
- 1 tsp curry powder
- 1 tbsp vegetable oil

Instructions:

1. Heat vegetable oil in a wok over medium-high heat. Add garlic and sauté until fragrant.
2. Add shrimp and chicken, cooking until they are cooked through.

3. Push the meat mixture to one side of the wok. Add beaten eggs to the other side and scramble until cooked.

4. Add rice, peas, carrots, pineapple, and cashews. Stir to combine.

5. Stir in soy sauce, fish sauce, oyster sauce, and curry powder. Cook for 2-3 more minutes.

6. Garnish with green onions and serve hot.

Stir-Fried Tofu with Shiitake Mushrooms

Ingredients:

- 1 block firm tofu, drained and cubed
- 1/2 lb shiitake mushrooms, sliced
- 1/2 onion, sliced
- 2-3 garlic cloves, minced
- 1 tbsp soy sauce
- 1 tbsp hoisin sauce
- 1 tbsp sesame oil
- 1 tbsp vegetable oil
- 1 tbsp rice vinegar
- 1 tsp sugar
- 2-3 green onions, chopped (for garnish)

Instructions:

1. Press the tofu to remove excess water, then cut it into cubes.
2. Heat vegetable oil in a wok or skillet over medium-high heat. Add tofu and sauté until golden brown on all sides. Remove tofu and set aside.
3. In the same wok, add sesame oil and sauté garlic, onions, and mushrooms until softened.
4. Stir in soy sauce, hoisin sauce, rice vinegar, and sugar. Add tofu back into the wok and toss to coat.

5. Cook for another 2-3 minutes, stirring occasionally.

6. Garnish with green onions and serve hot.

Chongqing Hot Chicken

Ingredients:

- 1 lb boneless, skinless chicken thighs, cut into bite-sized pieces
- 2 tbsp soy sauce
- 1 tbsp rice wine
- 1 tbsp cornstarch
- 1 tbsp vegetable oil
- 10-15 dried red chilies
- 1 tbsp Sichuan peppercorns
- 4-5 garlic cloves, minced
- 1-inch piece ginger, minced
- 2-3 green onions, chopped
- 1 tbsp sugar
- 1 tbsp soy sauce

Instructions:

1. Marinate the chicken pieces in soy sauce, rice wine, and cornstarch for 15-20 minutes.

2. Heat vegetable oil in a wok over medium-high heat. Add dried red chilies and Sichuan peppercorns, stirring until fragrant.

3. Add garlic, ginger, and chicken to the wok. Stir-fry for 5-7 minutes, until the chicken is cooked through.

4. Stir in sugar, soy sauce, and green onions. Cook for another 2-3 minutes.

5. Serve hot, garnished with more green onions if desired.

Spicy Garlic Crab

Ingredients:

- 2 crab legs, cracked and cleaned
- 2 tbsp vegetable oil
- 4-5 garlic cloves, minced
- 1-2 red chilies, chopped
- 1 tbsp soy sauce
- 1 tbsp chili paste
- 1 tbsp oyster sauce
- 1 tbsp rice wine
- 1 tsp sugar
- 2-3 green onions, chopped

Instructions:

1. Heat vegetable oil in a wok over medium-high heat. Add garlic and chilies, sautéing until fragrant.
2. Add crab legs and stir-fry for 2-3 minutes.
3. Stir in soy sauce, chili paste, oyster sauce, rice wine, and sugar. Cook for an additional 3-5 minutes until the crab is fully coated with the sauce.
4. Garnish with chopped green onions and serve immediately.

Salt and Pepper Squid

Ingredients:

- 1 lb squid, cleaned and cut into rings
- 1/2 cup cornstarch
- 1 tbsp black pepper
- 1 tbsp sea salt
- 1/2 tsp chili flakes (optional)
- 2-3 garlic cloves, minced
- 1 green onion, chopped
- 1 tbsp vegetable oil

Instructions:

1. In a bowl, combine cornstarch, black pepper, sea salt, and chili flakes.
2. Dredge the squid rings in the cornstarch mixture.
3. Heat vegetable oil in a frying pan over medium-high heat. Fry squid in batches until golden brown and crispy, about 2-3 minutes per batch.
4. Remove squid from oil and drain on paper towels.
5. In a separate pan, sauté garlic in a little oil until fragrant. Add the fried squid and toss to coat with the garlic.
6. Garnish with chopped green onions and serve.

Lo Mein with Vegetables

Ingredients:

- 8 oz lo mein noodles
- 1/2 cup carrots, julienned
- 1/2 cup bell peppers, thinly sliced
- 1/2 cup cabbage, shredded
- 1/4 cup snow peas
- 2-3 garlic cloves, minced
- 2 tbsp soy sauce
- 1 tbsp sesame oil
- 1 tbsp rice vinegar
- 1 tbsp hoisin sauce
- 1 tbsp vegetable oil
- 1 tsp sugar

Instructions:

1. Cook lo mein noodles according to package instructions. Drain and set aside.
2. Heat vegetable oil in a wok over medium-high heat. Add garlic and sauté until fragrant.
3. Add carrots, bell peppers, cabbage, and snow peas. Stir-fry for 2-3 minutes.

4. Add the cooked noodles to the wok along with soy sauce, sesame oil, rice vinegar, hoisin sauce, and sugar. Toss to combine.

5. Serve immediately.

Szechuan Shrimp

Ingredients:

- 1 lb shrimp, peeled and deveined
- 2 tbsp vegetable oil
- 2-3 garlic cloves, minced
- 1-inch piece ginger, minced
- 1 tbsp soy sauce
- 1 tbsp rice vinegar
- 1 tbsp chili paste
- 1 tbsp sugar
- 2-3 green onions, chopped
- 1/2 tsp ground Szechuan peppercorns

Instructions:

1. Heat vegetable oil in a wok over medium-high heat. Add garlic and ginger, cooking until fragrant.
2. Add shrimp and stir-fry for 3-4 minutes until pink and cooked through.
3. Stir in soy sauce, rice vinegar, chili paste, sugar, and ground Szechuan peppercorns.
4. Cook for an additional 2 minutes until the sauce thickens.
5. Garnish with green onions and serve.

Stir-Fried Eggplant with Minced Pork

Ingredients:

- 2 medium eggplants, cut into cubes
- 1/2 lb ground pork
- 2 tbsp soy sauce
- 1 tbsp hoisin sauce
- 1 tbsp rice wine
- 1 tbsp sugar
- 1-inch piece ginger, minced
- 2-3 garlic cloves, minced
- 1/2 cup chicken broth
- 2 tbsp vegetable oil
- 2-3 green onions, chopped (for garnish)

Instructions:

1. Heat vegetable oil in a wok over medium-high heat. Add ground pork and cook until browned.
2. Add garlic and ginger, sautéing until fragrant.
3. Stir in eggplant, soy sauce, hoisin sauce, rice wine, and sugar. Cook for 5-7 minutes until the eggplant is soft.
4. Add chicken broth and simmer for an additional 2-3 minutes until the sauce thickens.

5. Garnish with green onions and serve.

Crab Rangoon

Ingredients:

- 8 oz cream cheese, softened
- 1/2 cup crab meat (cooked or imitation)
- 1/4 cup green onions, chopped
- 1/2 tsp garlic powder
- 1/4 tsp soy sauce
- 1 pack wonton wrappers
- Vegetable oil for frying

Instructions:

1. In a bowl, mix cream cheese, crab meat, green onions, garlic powder, and soy sauce.
2. Place a small spoonful of the filling in the center of each wonton wrapper.
3. Wet the edges of the wrapper with water and fold into a triangle, sealing the edges tightly.
4. Heat vegetable oil in a pan over medium-high heat. Fry the wontons in batches for 2-3 minutes until golden and crispy.
5. Drain on paper towels and serve with sweet and sour sauce.

www.ingramcontent.com/pod-product-compliance
Lightning Source LLC
LaVergne TN
LVHW081618060526
838201LV00054B/2297